★　　★　　⌃　　▼　　✖

READER BONUS!

REFERRALS, REWARDS and REBATES

Thank you for reading this short book, which should not take more than an hour. I have a special reader bonus for you.

A bonus reward for referrals from this Book is 50% of the reward given to the author. For example, you receive $500 if the total reward is $1,000, when the installation is complete and as long as these programs last.

Just email the author at

jjsierra1937@gmail.com

with your name, zip code and email address. Your information is kept strictly confidential and not shared.

Also by Jon Cunningham

Around My Garden in 80 Years
Several articles in the International California
Mining Journal
Presentation At California Dental Association—
The First Yearlong USC Dental Implant Course

The Homeowner's Guide to
Purchasing Solar

$OLAR IN
$AN DIEGO

The Energy Enhancement Circle

JON CUNNINGHAM, DDS

For information about this title, contact the publisher:

4Paws Press, LLC
www.digdiego.com
jjsierra1937@gmail.com

060922

DISCLAIMER:

The information in this book is true and complete to the best of my knowledge. All recommendations are made without guarantee on the part of the author.

This book wasn't written for your exact situation. It is very important to do your own research and to follow all reasonable efforts to keep track of payments to the author and to yourself.

CONTENTS

DEDICATION

This book is dedicated to my wonderful wife, Joan. We met at Dana Junior High School in 1952. I was taken by her cute spunkiness and even more so when she offered to type my book reports and term papers. Seventy years later, she's still typing while I'm reading my very rough notes to her. All without pay! You make the Sun shine for me every day. I love you lots.

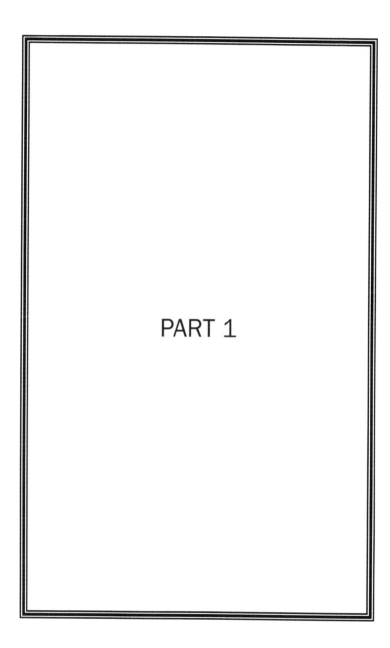

PART 1

WELCOME

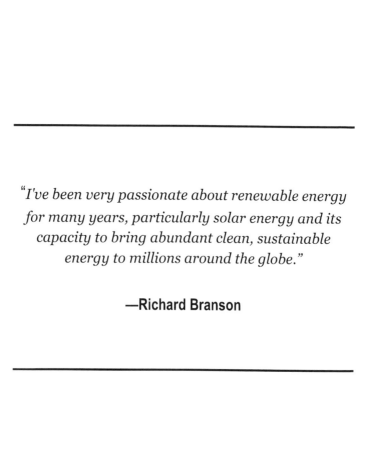

"I've been very passionate about renewable energy for many years, particularly solar energy and its capacity to bring abundant clean, sustainable energy to millions around the globe."

—Richard Branson

A DAUGHTER'S FOREWORD

For as long as I can remember, my dad has always had a strong connection with what I call Mother Earth...though I doubt he calls it that. Growing up, he was always eager to impart to us his knowledge of rock formations, mountain ranges, animal behaviors, sea life, etc. I could go on with countless stories from pet salamanders to coyote calls to climbing up a cliff face at Lake Powell and getting stuck up there while his two helpless children stared up from below.

All this adventuring with him instilled in me a love of nature, including plants and animals and the planet in general. I believe the impetus to write this book is his underlying love of Mother Nature and the beautiful planet we live on and his earnest desire to see it preserved for future generations.

Clean energy, specifically solar energy, is one of the keys to this. Thank you, Dad, for inspiring me to cherish our natural world and keep working to save our planet from the ravages of mankind. I hope this book inspires everyone who reads it to go solar.

—Jeri (Cunningham) Koltun

WELCOME

My wife, Joan, and I installed solar in 2018. The system we chose was a Power Purchase Agreement (PPA), which will be explained in a later chapter. We weren't sure what our total savings would be over our existing electric bill. After being on the system a couple of years, we were saving approximately 30% off the original electric bill, and we were very happy with the savings (see next page).

During that time, we referred a friend to the same company, but he chose to buy the entire system on time because his monthly payments were actually less than his former electric bill, which he no longer had to pay. Plus, he was able to take advantage of the government rebates and would be building equity in his home at the same time.

PRE-SOLAR BILL

Electricity Charges

Basic Service Charge	$7.85
Fuel Cost Charge	$14.98
Tier 1 Charge	$28.65
Tier 2 Charge	$84.65

Delivery Charges

Distribution Charge	$55.75
Transmission Charge	$46.88
Energy Commodity	$28.44
Energy Efficiency Charge	$8.42

Total: **$275.62**

POST-SOLAR BILL

Electricity Charges

Basic Service Charge	$7.85
Fuel Cost Charge	$0.00
Tier 1 Charge	$0.00
Tier 2 Charge	$0.00

Delivery Charges

Distribution Charge	$0.05
Transmission Charge	$0.00
Energy Commodity	$0.11
Energy Efficiency Charge	$0.23

Total: **$8.24**

When the salesperson gave us $1,000 cash for the referral, which came as a complete surprise, we immediately gave our friend $500 cash, and he was a happy camper.

Four years later, this solar company was bought out by another solar company who also gave us a $1,000 reward for referring another friend who we again gave $500 to.

Somewhere in the time period, we calculated that it would have been better for us to purchase the system on time or outright with cash. If we had purchased it on time, the overall savings over the long run would have been about 80%, and if we had paid cash, it would have been 99.9%.

We feel very strongly that the approach outlined in this book is a sensible method to counter the effects of climate change. It would be so easy to write a book on a single subject, such as solar, wind or water redistribution. However, all three topics are critical for our approach, so they will be used in combination. In the long run, wind, solar and hydro-electricity all complement each other, and in one form or another, will always be needed.

"If we use fuel to get our power, we are living on our capital and exhausting it rapidly. This method is barbarous and wantonly wasteful, and will have to be stopped in the interest of coming generations. The heat of the sun's rays represents an immense amount of energy."

—Nikola Tesla

WHO SHOULD READ
THIS BOOK?

This book assumes that most people are very interested in climate change and making some extra income. This was all explained in the front READER BONUS section.

"Clearly, we need more incentives to quickly increase the use of wind and solar power; they will cut costs, increase our energy independence and our national security and reduce the consequences of global warming."

—Hillary Rodham Clinton

MY PROMISE TO YOU

My promise to you is to make this a short, interesting and easily read book. It will probably take you about an hour to read. My first goal is to have the whole process of purchasing solar go smoothly for you. Along the way, you will learn how to both save and earn money.

My second goal is to spread the word, as I have mentioned in the Introduction. I promise that you will have a better understanding of what I call "The Energy Enhancement Circle."

THE ENERGY ENHANCEMENT CIRCLE

Making vehicle to grid (V2G) a reality will take some time, but it is coming.

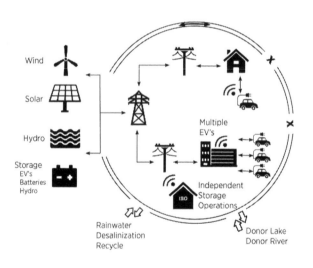

INTRODUCTION

The subtitle of this book "The Energy Enhancement Circle" refers to my ideal end point where I would like to end up some day. This means solar on as many roofs as possible, wind turbines and hydroelectric. These three solutions lead to clean energy for our planet. Getting there goes into a circle-like route and ties in with our huge water shortage problem.

The nuts and bolts in order to put all of this together would have to come from very high government levels. However, like the old saying, "The final result is much better than the sum of all its parts." What I am getting at is what past presidents and deep thinkers have accomplished.

For instance, President Teddy Roosevelt was the big motivator for the Panama Canal, and President Franklin D. Roosevelt was behind Social Security.

President John F. Kennedy got us to the Moon, and President Ronald Reagan, the "Great Communicator," helped tear down the Berlin Wall.

I would like to see a redistribution of water in the United States. Water, sun and air are all FREE and should belong to every person on Earth. Congress just approved a massive infrastructure bill, very little of which applied to our water problems. A lot of time and money would go into the following project, but the positive benefits would be enormous.

Water could be redistributed from areas where there is an abundance to areas that need it badly. Pipelines can be run along existing highways or railroad tracks, underground or above ground. They would run to large bodies of water, such as Lake Powell or Lake Oroville, where the pipes would run on the level or uphill. The water flow could be pushed by solar-powered pumps, where downhill you flow by gravity only.

For instance, water location and quantities could easily be taken care of with good software. If there was a drought on the East Coast, water could even be redistributed from the West Coast or possibly from Canada. I would think that dozens of large reservoirs with clean hydroelectric energy could be in operation year-round and even act as battery backup systems at night for utility-size solar systems.

The water could be used downstream from the dams for agriculture or general use. If there is excess water, it can be pumped back up to the lake using solar-powered pumps and used for more electricity generation.

This would have at least two major environmental enhancement aspects, which should make a lot of people happy.

Number one is that once the large reservoirs are all filled and balanced out, the hundreds of smaller dams could be removed, improving migration for salmon and steelhead trout.

The second one is that it would open up thousands of acres of previous land that was under water and restore it to its natural state. There are so many advantages of water redistribution that some of them will be covered in later chapters.

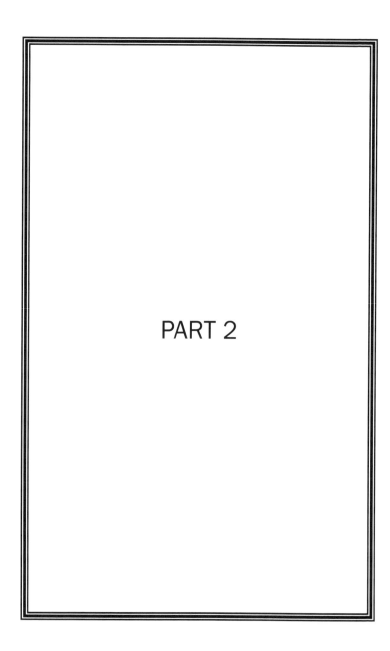

PART 2

SOLAR ESSENTIALS

"*We are like tenant farmers chopping down the fence around our house for fuel when we should be using Nature's inexhaustible sources of energy — sun, wind and tide.... I'd put my money on the sun and solar energy. What a source of power! I hope we don't have to wait until oil and coal run out before we tackle that.*"

—Thomas Edison

A SHORT HISTORY OF SOLAR

Our Earth revolves around the Sun, which is at the center of our solar system, 93 million miles away. The Sun is about 4.5 billion years old, and our closest estimation is that it has about another 4.5 billion years left in its life. The Sun is entirely gaseous, consisting of 74% hydrogen, 25% helium and 1% other elements. The light and heat given off by the Sun is caused by a constant nuclear chain reaction.

The history of solar is interesting and full of all sorts of characters, many famous and many not famous. It took a long time to develop solar technology as you will see in the following chronological order.

1839—Alexander Becquerel, a French physicist, discovered that light could produce an electric current under certain circumstances. He showed that when a semiconductor is exposed to sunlight, it generates an electric current.

1883—Charles Edgar Fritts built the first functioning solar electric module.

1890—The first rooftop solar was installed in New York. Fritts had used copper as a conductor and selenium as a semiconductor covered by a thin layer of gold leaf. However, the chemical properties of selenium were limited to 1%. This problem and the high cost of gold meant that these early solar modules were not commercially viable.

1905—Albert Einstein published his theories of subatomic particles and the photoelectric effects. Einstein's discovery of protons and the electric current produced by semiconductors were what brought everything together.

1954—Bell Telephone Laboratories developed a more efficient semiconductor than selenium, which turned out to be silicone, a very common element that makes up sand and quartz.

1964—Bell Labs started producing solar cells from silicone. The price of solar was not practical for most consumers due to the high cost of purifying silicone and module manufacturing capabilities. Federal support for development of solar cells for space satellites was strong, but high costs persisted through the 1960's even though conversion efficiencies reached 14%.

1970's—Fossil fuels' costs worried even the oil companies about future fuel shortages. They were motivated to do research for alternative fuel sources, including solar. The big breakthrough was when a chemist named Elliott Berman approached Exxon Oil. Berman had determined that impurities in silicon crystals did not greatly reduce their solar capabilities' efficiencies. He uses leftover silicon that had been used in the semiconductor industry. This reduced the cost of solar cell manufacturing from $100 to $20 per cell. Around the same time, Exxon started making solar panels to provide electricity for water pumps for their oil wells, and these first panels were much more affordable. Solar cell prices dropped by 80%, and this continued into the early 2000's.

CRITICAL ENERGY POLICY

A second wave of renewable energy growth was fueled by energy policy, which had a huge impact on the solar industry. Local, state and federal policies encouraged or required development of renewable energy.

President Nixon Administration—produced "Project Independence" for the U.S. to have energy independence by 1980.

President Gerald Ford—passed five energy-related bills. One of which was the Energy Tax Act of 1978 that created the Solar Investment Tax Credit

(ITC). This provided huge financial support to the solar industry.

President Jimmy Carter—enacted a very important bill affecting the solar industry. This was the Public Utilities Regulatory Policy Act (PURPA). An important part of this legislation involved enactment of net metering.

President Ronald Reagan—had a goal to reduce the business burdens, which resulted in decreasing many of the incentives that had already been passed. He removed the solar panels on the White House. All this almost wiped out the wind and solar industries. During this same period, he was known as the Great Communicator and should get credit for removing the Berlin Wall.

President Barack Obama—following the 2008 financial crash, passed the American Recovery and Reinvestment Act of 2009. This removed the cap on the Investment Tax Credit and effectively reduced the cost of solar by 30%. This transformed the solar industry as a whole.

President Donald Trump—did not believe in climate change and reversed most of the incentives for renewable energy and nixed the Paris Climate Accord.

President Joe Biden—is a strong believer in climate change as I am and 99% of all world scientists. He reversed most of Trump's changes and renewed the Paris Climate Accord.

"*There has been a systematic repression of solar energy. It seems pretty funny to me that the government, if it is completely neutral—why wouldn't they pursue this far safer alternative of solar energy with the same intent that they pursue nuclear energy?*
Solar power is the last energy resource that isn't owned yet—nobody taxes the sun yet."

—Bonnie Raitt

CHOOSING SOLAR OPTIONS

In 2005, the Investment Tax Credit (ITC) was reintroduced. At that time, a new program called third party ownership (TPO) came into the solar industry. It was meant to get the financial benefits of solar without investing large sums of money. The main idea behind the TPO was a contract called a power purchase agreement (PPA).

Power Purchase Agreement (PPA): This made solar available to millions of homeowners who do not have thousands of dollars to purchase solar. The customer agrees to pay for the electricity generated by the solar equipment by a third party who pays for the equipment and installation. The third party retains ownership of the solar system. The homeowner pays a monthly solar bill, which covers the cost of the electricity they generate. They also lock in a fixed electricity rate, which is much lower than the ever-increasing utility rates. The contract is usually for 20 years, by which time the system is usually paid for. The customer actually pays the solar service company a lower and more predictable rate over the utilities company's rates.

The Solar Lease: If you sign a PPA, you can also lease equipment. However, under these two circumstances, the homeowners do not own the system. Under the PPA or the Solar Lease, the average savings is usually around 30%, but you can't take advantage of the rebate program. However, since you are not the owner, maintenance is up to the solar company.

The Solar Loan: These are becoming more popular than the PPAs because many customers don't just want to take advantage of these PPA savings; they also want to receive all of the financial incentives of ownership, such as the Investment Tax Credit and deductibles. Many banks and solar companies make solar loans. Again, it only makes good sense to use the money normally paid for electricity on your utility bill to make payments for your solar system.

Cash Purchase: Even though cash is still king and allows all the advantages of full ownership, many people would rather save their cash and use it for other purposes.

Whether you're buying with a solar loan or paying cash, don't forget the federal tax credit is 26% throughout 2022 and 22% throughout 2023 and unless it is reinstated is 0% after 2024.

"America is home to the best researchers, advanced manufacturers, and entrepreneurs in the world. There is no reason we cannot lead the planet in manufacturing solar panels and wind turbines, engineering the smart energy grid, and inspiring the next great companies that will be the titans of a new green energy economy."

—Brad Schneider

CHOOSING A SOLAR COMPANY

As mentioned, it is very important to compare apples to apples when choosing a solar company whether it's local, regional or national. If you do your research online, quite often the information is misleading. Be sure to check the contract fine print, including warranties and rewards for referrals. And be sure you are happy with the salesperson's approach and how long the whole process takes. My personal opinion is to not just choose the cheapest company but choose the less expensive bid as long as you feel the installer is trustworthy and you feel comfortable with the overall picture.

When talking to neighbors or friends, find out who they used and if they were very happy with the company. Before we signed our contract, we had checked with five neighbors and friends who had the same options and were all very happy. One of these people recently sold their house, and the transfer of the PPO option went smoothly with no problems.

LOOKING BACK

Almost everything we use these days requires electricity. I'm able to say things to my grandchildren, such as, *"Why, when I was your age, I used to go to my grandparents' house and their telephone was mounted on the wall. I could even listen in to the neighbors talking on their phone on the 'party line.' Then came the dial phone, then the push button and now the cell phone. No more wires."*

I can also look back to when we moved to Los Angeles, and they had just stopped incinerators burning trash in people's backyards. However, this did not get rid of the smog problem, and I can remember looking forward to having to stop at a red light so I could close my eyes as they would be stinging so badly from the smog. Not until automobile catalytic converters were required did the problem start to get resolved.

"If you hate me and you hate the government, solar energy is for you. Because you'll make your own electricity."

—Bill Nye ("the Science Guy")

LOOKING FORWARD

Almost every change these days seems to involve electricity, namely solar, wind, hydroelectric or storage. Many countries, including China, are working hard to bring climate change under control. California, as usual, is leading the pace of change in the U.S., and here are some of the changes taking place at present.

Stanford University has just developed a solar panel that produces electricity at night. The amount of power produced is quite low, but I'm sure this will be improved. Many entrepreneurs are working on solar panels that can be used in space where the Sun always shines, and the power can be beamed back to Earth by radio waves.

Battery storage and net metering technologies are constantly changing. The latest being you can plug in your electric vehicle at home. And when it's not in use, its battery power storage can be used by the grid for many purposes, such as instant electricity needed for emergencies, off- or on-peak uses.

With the new artificial intelligence and smart software, it's all kept track of to pay you automatically in dollars. This software can also keep track of your driving habits and when your car is being used.

California now has over one million all-electric vehicles (EVs), and multiplying this by tens of millions of EVs in the future is very impressive. So, with everyone's EV connected, it's like one giant battery. We are getting better at keeping track of carbon dioxide emissions and the progress we are making toward climate change.

11

NET METERING

Net metering is the process by which our utility company keeps track of how much electricity we use or need. Like a bank account, if we make more electricity than we use, it's given back to us at the present going rate of electricity.

Ongoing California Legislative talks may decrease the amount paid to the homeowner. The thinking is that solar system owners are being overpaid because they are favored over the non-solar owning citizens and that they need to pay some extra money for infrastructure, etc.

"I know that solar electric works. How do I know that? Because it's been making my electricity since 1990...These things work. We need to embrace them as quickly as possible."

—Ed Begley Jr.

COMMUNITY CHOICE
PROGRAMS (CCP)

The reasoning behind Community Choice Programs is to generate electricity through more environmentally friendly sources, such as solar, hydroelectric and wind, instead of the usual utility-sourced electricity. California, being the hotbed of innovation that it is, has several of the programs going, and they all have different features and benefits and are still to be proven.

One of the best things about CCP is the fact that large-scale programs allow lower-cost electricity to go to much of the population that either can't afford solar or live in areas that can't be served by solar, such as some apartment buildings. One of the negative aspects of large-scale solar programs is that they are not very environmentally friendly because it covers up a lot of the vegetation and affects wildlife also.

Some CCPs, depending on the particular community, automatically enroll the utility customers, and if they don't want to participate, they can opt out. Other CCP programs are structured so that if you want to join, you can opt in. The programs are not going to save the customers a lot of money, possibly 1% at the most, and are still a work in progress. Some CCPs are more successful than others. And at least one county had to file for bankruptcy.

San Diego County recently went through the following steps: San Diego Gas & Electric had been our only provider for about 50 years. In 2021, their contract ran out, so the City of San Diego tried to build a more competitive environment by soliciting other players. This did not work out because nobody applied, and the city had no choice but to stay with SDG&E.

San Diego's CCP version came to be. And in its version, all of SDG&E's customers were automatically enrolled into the CCP with the option of, if you didn't want to be in it, you had to opt out. Again, the approximate savings was 1% also.

Again, a large percentage of CCP customers would be better off taking the money they would normally pay for electricity to their utility company and using it for monthly payments on their own rooftop system. Regarding what it says in Chapter 5 about electric vehicles acting as battery storage means you will likely not need to have a separate battery backup, which will give you the choice of being grid free or net metering and staying on the grid.

"We have this handy fusion reactor in the sky called the sun. You don't have to do anything, it just works. It shows up every day."

—Elon Musk

ELON MUSK

Elon Musk was born in Pretoria, South Africa. He's often referred to as a visionary comparable to Steve Jobs of Apple. He is the CEO of Tesla, Inc. and has contributed considerably to helping climate change. Tesla has become the largest electric vehicle company in the world.

The Model 3, as with the previous models, is a wonderful EV, made of aluminum, and the battery pack being in the center and down low makes it very safe by the American National Safety Standards Institute. The cost is in the mid to high range, depending on the model.

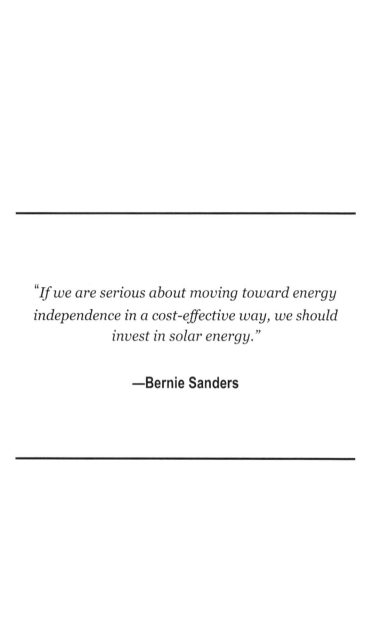

"*If we are serious about moving toward energy independence in a cost-effective way, we should invest in solar energy.*"

—Bernie Sanders

SAVING JOBS

It will come as a reassuring message to all future workers in the renewable energy field that their jobs are probably secure for many years. If 90% of the population had rooftop solar, the large-scale utilities will still be needed. I would hope they would become smaller and less needed in future years. However, the fact that millions of cars can be used for battery storage means income for the EV owners and the utilities, and last but not least, the utility stock holders.

"I mean, the electric car is here to stay. I predict a child born today will probably drive in a gasoline-powered car about as often as you would drive in a car with a stick shift."

—Jay Leno

ELECTRIC VEHICLES (EV) ARE SELLING LIKE HOTCAKES!

Everyone has a different viewpoint about the environment or our dependence on foreign oil. EVs offer so much better acceleration with much less cost than internal combustion cars.

On that point, my friend Mark gets a new car every week to test drive and writes about it on his website: MaynardsGarage.com. Recently, he had a Hyundai Ioniq to analyze. This EV is not only fun and easy to drive but also beautifully designed. It really took my breath away. The only problem is it's so popular that potential customers can't even reserve them. Hopefully, that will change soon.

My neighbor recently gave me a ride in his Tesla Model 3. This car is impeccable in every aspect. You would be hard-pressed to find a car where everything

ELECTRIFIED VEHICLE SALES
2020 VS. 2021

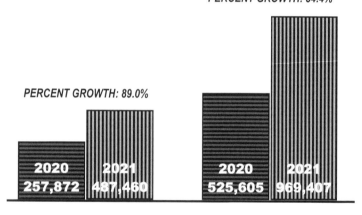

PERCENT GROWTH: 84.4%

PERCENT GROWTH: 89.0%

2020
257,872

2021
487,460

2020
525,605

2021
969,407

Electric vehicles (EVs)

Hybrid electric and plug-in
vehicles (HEVs and PHEVs)

Source: Kelley Blue Book

is laid out as nicely, including the flush door handles and the 15" touchscreen computer monitor.

My final choice was to buy my next-door neighbor's 1987 Chevrolet El Camino, which I plan to convert to an EV. The price was fair, and the overall costs with me doing most of the work will be very reasonable. This should be a real learning experience but made easier because of all the help from the internet and books available on the subject.

Removed from the original pickup will be the old motor, transmission, AC and almost everything under the hood including the radiator. This will leave plenty of space for the new, very small electric motor and batteries. These cars are totally silent and should be fun and impress all my rowdy friends.

The most recent big EV news is the Mercedes Benz Vision EQXX EV that set a new distance record of almost 700 miles on a single charge. Have fun!

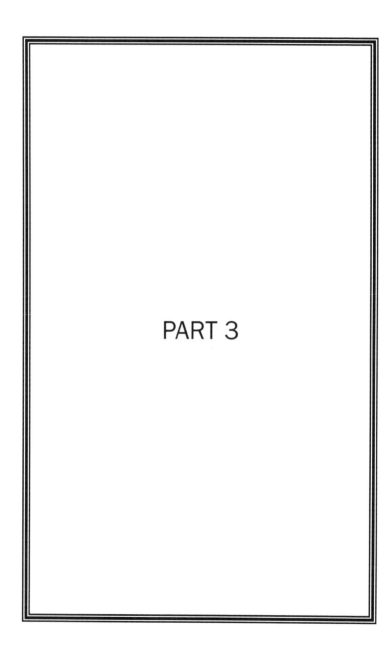

PART 3

THE PATH FORWARD

"I think it is important for all of us to do our little part to make the world cleaner. The impact goes beyond just saving money."

—Jon Cunningham

THE NEXT STEP

Congratulations on making it through this book, and thank you for reading it. At this point, I hope you now have a better understanding of how solar works.

If you wish to go further, please email me at jjsierra1937@gmail.com with your name, zip code and email address. I will send you a few names of solar companies, some of which pay for referrals and some which do not. Please do your own research to determine which company you wish to use. Don't be shy about asking if any particular company pays for referrals and tell them that you will be splitting with us if they in fact do give referral rewards. Solar companies sometimes come and go but most of them are good and solid. Our comfort level with these companies comes from personal experience or talking to the owners and their customers. Again, don't be shy about asking any particular company to give you names of people they have helped.

Hopefully, this book will bring you up to speed on what to look for in not only choosing the correct financial option but the correct company as well. You might consider talking to your neighbors and friends as we did, which helped our thinking considerably. I do think it would be a good idea if you wish to make some more money to do exactly what I'm requesting you to do in this book. In other words, refer your friends, and you will get rewarded.

ABOUT JON CUNNINGHAM

I was born and raised in San Diego. During my three years at Point Loma High School, I spent summers tuna fishing off of Baja and Mexico. I then went to dental school at USC, and then worked on patients at the Monterey Defense Language Institute and Naval Postgraduate School in the Monterey area for two years.

I then returned to San Diego and practiced with my father and oldest son, Grey, both USC dentists for many years. Interestingly, we have a triplet grandchild who will graduate from high school next year and is talking about attending USC dentistry school also. If so, she will probably be the first fourth generation Herman Ostrow School of Dentistry of USC graduate. During this time, I married my high school sweetheart, and we raised four children in a house we built near Point Loma High School.

Other interests along the way, I flew various aircraft and raced a small sailboat for many years. I was very involved with Cub and Webelos Scouts and Lions Club helping the blind. I am a Life member of the American Dental Association, California Dental Association and San Diego County Dental Society.

NOTES

READER BONUS!

REFERRALS, REWARDS and REBATES

Thank you for reading this short book, which should not take more than an hour. I have a special reader bonus for you.

A bonus reward for referrals from this Book is 50% of the reward given to the author. For example, you receive $500 if the total reward is $1,000, when the installation is complete and as long as these programs last.

Just email the author at

jjsierra1937@gmail.com

with your name, zip code and email address. Your information is kept strictly confidential and not shared.

Made in the USA
Middletown, DE
22 June 2022